Trap

Contents

Titles in the Runway series

Level 4	Level 5	Level 6
The Street	Trapped	The Good Student
The Wish	The Rumour	Virtual Teacher
The Magic Shop	The Food Museum	Football Smash
The Ghost House	Escape from the City	The Empty House

Badger Publishing Limited
15 Wedgwood Gate, Pin Green Industrial Estate,
Stevenage, Hertfordshire SG1 4SU
Telephone: 01438 356907. Fax: 01438 747015
www.badger-publishing.co.uk
enquiries@badger-publishing.co.uk

Trapped ISBN 978 1 84691 371 6

Publisher: David Jamieson
Commissioning Editor: Carrie Lewis
Design: Fiona Grant
Illustration: Robin Lawrie, Aleksandar Sotirovski, Anthony Williams

Printed and bound in China through Colorcraft Ltd., Hong Kong

>>Trapped ____

Written by **Alison Hawes**
Illustrated by **Robin Lawrie**

Kim and Stefan were looking for money.
They were not looking at the sea.

The sea came in very quickly.
They had to climb onto the rocks.

The sea got higher and higher.
Stefan called for help.
He called 999.
But it was no good.
He could not get a signal.

The sea got higher and higher.
Kim and Stefan had to climb up the cliff.

The sea got higher and higher.
But Kim and Stefan could not climb higher.
It was no good.
They were trapped!

Then Kim saw a man at the top of the cliff.
They called for help.

But it was no good.
The man could not
hear them.

Then Stefan had an idea.
He turned the old coin in the sun.
The man saw the coin flash in the sun.
He saw Kim and Stefan.

The man called for help.
He called 999.

SOS

Written by Melanie Joyce
Illustrated by Aleksander Sotirovski

The orb flashed suddenly.
Dax and Tess vanished.
The orb vanished.
The crew were alone.

It was dark, but Dax and Tess saw something move.

Where are we?

I don't know.

Something growled behind Dax and Tess. Something with claws suddenly grabbed Dax.

Tess, run!

Tess ran into the dark.
She sent the SOS.

I've got to send an SOS to the crew. 6.4.2.5.5

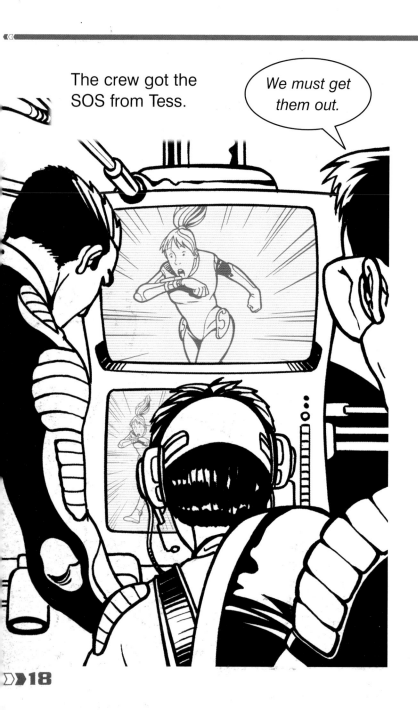

18

The crew got the
SOS from Tess.
We must get them out.

Tess waited for help from the crew.
Suddenly Dax was back.

Tess. Help me!

999 ««

Written by Stan Cullimore
Illustrated by Anthony Williams

Ian and Sairah were in the park.
Sairah got out her mobile phone.

Ian climbed a tree.
Sairah sent texts on her mobile phone.

Suddenly Ian shouted to Sairah,
"We must help him!"

"Who must we help?" said Sairah.

"A car has hit a man on a motorbike.
The man is on the floor. He looks hurt,"
said Ian.

Sairah rang 999 on her mobile phone.
"Help. A car has hit a man on a motorbike."

The ambulance came. The paramedics got out.
"He is not breathing," said a paramedic.

The paramedic put his lips to the man's lips.
He breathed into his mouth.

The man opened his eyes.
"You saved my life," he said.

"Sairah and Ian saved your life by ringing 999," said the paramedic.

>>> Vocabulary

Trapped

coin
quickly
climb
rocks
signal
cliff
trapped
idea
turned
flash

SOS

orb
touch
suddenly
vanished
crew
growled
claws
grabbed

999

climbed
tree
texts
suddenly
shouted
motorbike
floor
hurt
rang
ambulance
paramedic
breathing
mouth

⏩⏩ Story questions

Trapped

What did Stefan and Kim find?
How did they try to get away from the sea?
Who did the man on the cliff call?

SOS

Why did Dax and Tess vanish?
What happens to Dax in the dark?
What do you think will happen to the crew?

999

What does Ian see from the tree?
What does Sairah do to help?
How does the paramedic help the man?